Key
Images

Acknowledgement of Complimentary Book
We are happy to present this review copy of our new book:

We'd appreciate two copies of your review. Also notify us of the date you plan to review our book and the reviewer. If you don't plan to review our book please let us know why. Please return all correspondence to:

Distinctive Publishing Corp.
P.O. Box 17868
Plantation, FL 33318-7868

SANDY FINK

dp

DISTINCTIVE PUBLISHING CORP.

Key Images
By Sandy Fink
Copyright 1992 by Sandy Fink

Published by Distinctive Publishing Corp.
P.O. Box 17868
Plantation, Florida 33318-7868
Printed in the United States of America

All rights reserved. No part of this book may be reproduced, stored in a retrieval system, or transmitted, in any form or by any means, electronic, mechanical, photocopying, recording, or otherwise, without the written permission of the publisher.

ISBN: 0-942963-16-4
Library of Congress No.: 91-71743
Price: $9.95

Dedication

Dedicated to the place and to its population of people and other creatures; and to the proposition that not all places are created equal; and to the premise that not all places have the power to so profoundly touch and test us with life surrounded by sun and sea.

ABOUT THE AUTHOR

Sandy Fink has been published, as a poet, nationally, in small press and other literary magazines; her work appears in an anthology and several chapbooks. She has been published as a freelance writer, humorist, columnist and creator of children's puzzles. She is a member of Florida Freelance Writers Association, South Florida Poets' Association, and the Oregon State Poets' Association. Sandy lives with her husband, grown son, two dogs and three cats at Big Pine Key, Florida.

TABLE OF CONTENTS

Images of Key West	9
Key Deer	10
The Monogram Tree	11
Coral Kaleidoscope	12
Mangroves	13
The Sun	14
The Tourist Tree	15
Fisherman's Shack	16
Sea Oats	17
The Leaf-Size Lizards of Big Pine Key	18
Frigatebirds	19
Mamma Manatee	20
Hawks	21
Moving Images	22
Accommodation	23
Fat Fish	24
The Sea	25
The Ibis	26
Gathering Storms	27
A Beacon	28
Links	29
Collectors	30
Midnight Moonlight	31
Sailing	32
Clouds	33

Paradoxical Nourishment	34
A Tropical Wind	35
Midnight Beach	36
People Places	37
Coconuts	38
Sunshine Sand Dancers	39
The Heron	40
Sea Tongues	41
Big Pine Key Deer	42
Thomas Jefferson's Dream Come True	43
Midnight Sand Dancers	44
The Storm	45
Gulls	46
Keys Sun	47
Survivor	48
On Someone's Hook	49
Big Bad John Of Big Pine Key	50
Key Turtles	51
Born To Be	52
Two Dolphins	53
Waves	54
Marlin	55
A Conch Knows	56
Wildlife Preservation	57
The Blue Hole At Night	58
A Dying Pine Tree	59
Something Sounds Fishy	60
Sunset Sea Dancers	61
May Through September	62

Images of Key West

Conch trains and Old Town tours,
The Hemmingway House, the in-town
                                  lighthouse,
Mallory Market with its
                         sunset crowds,

Sloppy Joes.
Old-world streets and clapboard houses,
Gingerbread-trimmed and painted
                            white.
Mopeds, t-shirts, conch shells —
Everything for rent or sale.
Hotels and condos, rising white and
                           shiny, from the sea.
Palmy beaches with resident seagulls
Patrolling with squawking glides.
Ships at dock, freighters on the horizon,
Every size and shape
Houseboat, fishing boat, sailboat, yacht
Tied to pelican-deco docks and wharves.
And, of course, sunrise and sunset —
That sacramental soul of a city
Like no other.

Key Deer

Setting suns still rise
On miniature Key deer
Whose days seem numbered.

The Monogram Tree

When you come to visit me,
You'll write your name
And the date you came
To Big Pine Key,
On a leaf of a growing
Monogram tree.

Coral Kaleidoscope

Beyond sun-kissed aqua swallows,
In the bright blue world of the
              deep reef,
Flowers of stone reach for sunshine,
While feathers and fans dance
              with water.
And fish, eccentrically costumed
For life-and-death games of
              hide and seek,
Find perfect shelter there, among
Marvelously colorful coral.

Mangroves

Shiny-leafed and green,
Mangroves line each curving coast,
Catching muffled waves.

Treasures of the sea
Are captured and kept there, in
Shadows and stillness.

Palm fronds, coconuts,
Abandoned crab and conch shells
And seaweed gather.

Ripples of waves touch
Hidden places and nourish
Living things, hiding.

Regal white egret,
Standing in a mangrove swamp
Knows each hiding place.

The Sun

The sun that moves through palms
                with grace
And warms a puppy's upturned face,
Can quickly turn both bark and bone
To sun-bleached stone.

The Tourist Tree

Bursera, bitterwood,
West Indian birch,
Gumbo Limbo —
So many names
Can leave one reeling.
But anyone who lives
On a Florida Key,
Calls Gumbo Limbo
The tourist tree —
And with feeling.
After all, it is
Always red and peeling.

Fisherman's Shack

Give me a shack
With room to stack
My fishing gear
Nearer than near
To the sea.

Instead of a clock,
Give me a dock
And a boat to stay
Out of harms way
Close to me.

Sea Oats

Soft breezes play
In the sun-kissed sand,
Among perennial grasses
Grown tall in hot, dry, salty places
That would kill most living things.
Sea oats more than survive and thrive
At the fragile edge of terra firma.
A hearty stand of sea oats
Helps protect a beach from wind and wave.
Like the best of us, they create a better world
Just being there, where they are
Because of what they are.

The Leaf-size Lizards of Big Pine Key

The chameleons and geckos we always see
Are the leaf-size lizards of Big Pine Key.
They are cute (well, as cute as lizards can be).
But, what if these tiny lizards grew
To twice the size of an over-size shoe?
And, what if they grew as dragons do
In fact and fantasy? Would we ignore
A huge tropical lizard carnivore?

frigatebirds

Hooked-wing frigate-birds
Ride air currents above me,
Beyond me, to where?

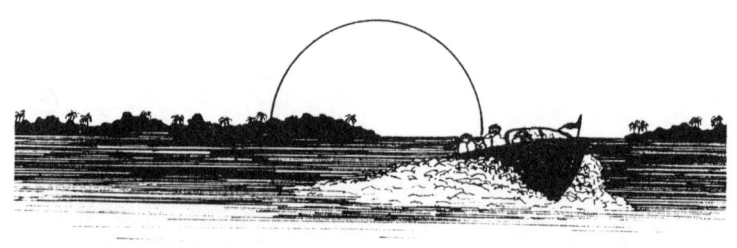

Mamma Manatee

Beyond debate,
It's much too late
For mamma manatee.
We can not wait,
Or mamma's fate
Will also find her baby.
Fatal features
Of these gentle creatures
Are found in how they trust us.
In sight, hindsight
Creates more justice.

Hawks

Shadows squat in sun
So startling bright — even
Reflected light burns.

Stark white bones of tree
Are sclerotic testaments
To time, sun and sea.

White heron feed in
Deer shadows — on bugs and such
Stirred up in grazing.

Hawks slide through the sky,
Scouring scrubbrush, sinkholes,
Mangrove swamps for food.

They cast small shadows
Crossing buttonwood hammocks
And fresh-water pines.

Coons sleep in shadows —
So do snakes, lizards and frogs.
They wait for darkness.

Moving Images

Moving images
Are caught within reflected
Sun-filled sea shallows.

Colorful fish feed
Among colorful coral —
And are fed upon.

The sunshine sparkles
Each blue and green jeweled crest
Of lively water.

Shadows, large and small,
Move beneath those busy waves —
Still stalking and stalked.

A spectacular
Sun begins and ends each day
With or without one.

Accommodation

Between road and sea —
Utility poles, topped with
Shy nesting osprey.

Fat fish, fat fish,
Come take my hook.
I need to hook a fish
To have a fish to cook.

The Sea

The tumult of a seething sea
Irrevocably calls me.
Terrified, I may be
Temporarily free
From some lifetime sea
That swallowed me.

The Ibis

We live our lives on Big Pine Key,
And I can not help but smile
To know who comes to visit me
The Ibis of the Nile.

Gathering Storms

No wisps of cloud
For a Florida Key —
No whispering rains; but
Banks of cumulonimbus
That bump and thunder
In noisy charges
Across an aqua sea,
Touched by gods who left behind
Thumbprints of land beneath
Gathering storms.

A Beacon

He stands, a beacon
In a swirling storm, pouring
Light into darkness.

Links

Land-linking bridges
Between islands became our
Umbilical cord.

Our survival hangs
On fragile threads we weave and
Hand to God, in trust,

While we work and play
Near the sea, on the sea and
Mostly in the sun.

Collectors

Some collect antiques, books,
    clowns, coins, stamps
(Whatever seems significant enough
To warrant personal collection),
And store them here, there — where ever.
I collect sunsets, clouds, unaccountably
    sweet moments,
And store them, handy,
In my mind.

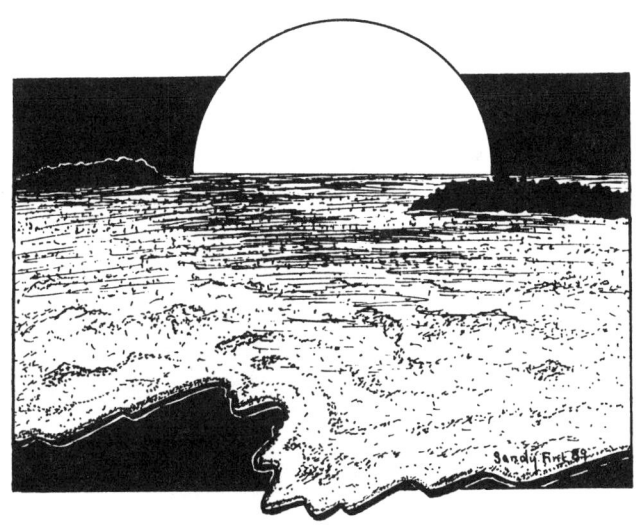

Midnight Moonlight

Something magical
Happens to me
When midnight moonlight
Dances across a
 tropical sea.

Sailing

Sailing, sunrise
To sunset, savoring sun,
Sea and salty spray.

Mostly feeling free
While in control, knowing
Each strength and weakness.

Clouds

The Florida Keys
Sprout and grow marvelously
Large mushrooms of clouds.

I could spend my life
In sunshine-touched shadows of
Clouds that come and grow.

Paradoxical Nourishment

Short, scrubby brushwood
Dip tender tap roots into
Salt water and lime.

And new life begins
Among the toughened stilt roots
Of sun-kissed mangroves.

A Tropical Wind

A tropical wind
Will scream historically
Between the whispers.

Midnight Beach

Slivers and slices
Of moonshine ~ or full moons ~ play
On paradise Keys.

Palm trees, caressed by
Balmy, tropical breezes,
Rustle, soft and sweet.

Salty, coral sand,
Still filled with full-shell fossils,
Is warm at midnight.

People Places

Restaurants, condos,
Warehouses, other buildings
Hug and kiss the sea.

Sea gulls gather there,
Where wavelets ripple the shore —
Glide, soar, do wheelies.

Silver-grey wharves are
Decorated with at-home
Fat, brown pelicans.

Tugs, freighters and ships
Move along the horizon,
Slow sea denizens.

Tiny boats ride — rise
And fall — on the dark blue waves
While storm clouds gather.

Coconuts

Critters who live on the Florida Keys,
Can grow and gather nuts with ease,
But only off the coconut trees.

Sunshine Sand Dancers

Chattering sea gulls
Gather, leave ~ gather again ~
Sunshine sand dancers.

The Heron

Still, shallow water —
A sun-kissed heron, drinking
Its own reflection.

Sea Tongues

Soft aqua sea tongues
Lick parched lips of sandy beach
Again and again.

Endlessly touching,
The sea gives up some treasure
And so does the beach.

Gentle caresses
Can become awesome attacks
With death, destruction.

Big Pine Key Deer

Miniature Key deer,
Gathered at dusk, do not know
their shrinking numbers.

Thomas Jefferson's Dream-Come-True

Thomas Jefferson
Made a dream come true;
And Fort Jefferson,
America's largest coastal fort
Rose on a mucky island
Seventy miles from Key West,
In the vast waters
Of the Gulf of Mexico.
Built by slaves and prisoners,
It lives on, a testament
To dreams come true.
Obsolete before
The last brick was set,
It protected nothing,
Attacked no one;
And nothing can protect
Fort Jefferson from
Wind, water and time.

Midnight Sand Dancers

Slender-trunk palm trees
Slice the moon at odd angles —
Midnight sand dancers.

The Storm

Rumbling thunder moves through
Packed clouds piled high, spread low.
A wind whips through the shallows,
Clouding aqua clearness with silt.
Boats bob on bristled, slate-grey seas,
Moved with ominous tension; they
Slice through burly crests and eddies,
                        heading home.
Lightning, that frenzied dancer, leaps
                        back and forth
Across a dimmed and deserted stage
Even sea gulls and pelicans
Have left to the storm.

Gulls

Gulls, in syncopated flight,
Scramble, scrappy, in descent
To a scuffled, sun-scorched sea,
Scattering cries to the wind.

Keys Sun

Silver sun, gold sun —
Or the orange-red sun that
Sinks into the sea.

Survivor

Nothing survived those
Wild winds, whole, except a
Fragile spider web.

On Someone's Hook

Seems like every where I look
There is a fish on someone's hook.
Swimming fish seem better than
Fish sizzling in my frying pan.

PS: This poem is NOT about fish.

Big Bad John
of Big Pine Key

Special places
Draw special people,
Most of us will agree.
When time erases
All but traces
Of you and of me,
Many Key folks will still
Recall Big Bad John
Of Big Pine Key.

Key Turtles

Impenetrable
Armor should have protected
Key turtles — and you.

Born to Be

You, swirling storm in tropical seas, were born to be a hurricane.

Two Dolphins

In lyric silence,
Two dolphins play, touched gently
By jeweled water.

Waves

Waves rise with the wind,
Beat and batter my boat. I
Trust it's seaworthy.

Marlin

Marlin leap, dance on
Water, disappear — shadows
Of their former selves.

A Conch Knows

They never wait for a sky that grieves,
Or barometric pressures that spell
                            their doom.
When too many poinciana trees
Lose their leaves ~ or fail to bloom ~
When butterflies and bees
Won't land but circle, around and
                            around;
When land crabs move to higher ground,
And ants seem to crawl straight up
                            a wall;
When dogs and cats and birds seem touched
By a non-existant full moon,
Conchs know ~ or actively assume ~
A hurricane is coming
Very soon.

Wildlife Preservation

Audubon, a man
Whose name is synonymous
With wildlife preservation,
Had no interest in the
Survival of birds —
Except on paper.
He killed them tirelessly
For sport, amusement and art.
And preservation of birds
For Audubon meant stuffing them
In lifelike positions, because
He wanted to capture them
More lifelike on paper —
At leisure.

The Blue Hole at Night

Alligators are
Primeval armor-plated
Kin of dinosaurs.

A crotchety beast,
Seemingly all jaws and tail,
Sinks in black water.

Our flashlight captures
Blood-red eyes ~ by the dozens ~
Watching us at night.

Poisonwood branches
Brush water. Night fills with an
Unquiet stillness.

An owl punctuates
Loud staccato passages
Of tropical frogs.

The air is heavy,
Filled with fragrances and rot ~
No seabreeze tonight.

In the frail moonlight
Soft splashes and then silence;
Water grasses move.

A Dying Pine Tree

A dying pine tree
Scatters the earth beneath it
With seeded pine cones.

Something Sounds Fishy

Something sounds fishy about a story
With all the struggle and, then, the glory
That begins with a fisherman's wish
And ends with a fisherman's fish.

Sunset Sea Dancers

Gently bobbing boats,
Anchored, ride wide golden waves ~
Sunset sea dancers.

May Through September

Visit the Keys, and you'll know, too,
That clouds pile up like the Devil's
own brew.

Note from the author: Thanks for joining me for a taste of some of what makes the Florida Keys such a special place to visit for a few days — or for a lifetime.

To order additional copies of *Key Images* by Sandy Fink, send $9.95 plus $3.00 shipping and handling for each copy ordered to:

Distinctive Publishing Corp.
P.O. Box 17868
Plantation, Florida 33318-7868

Quantity discounts available.